ORGANOID INTELLIGENCE: AN INTRODUCTION

Dr Charlie Barnes

ISBN: 9798345313480

Cover design by: Dave Price

CONTENTS

INTRODUCTION

Organoid Intelligence: The Future of Computing?

The human brain is an incredible organ. It allows us to think, learn, remember, and experience the world around us. The complexity and capabilities of the brain are truly awe-inspiring. But what if we could harness this power for computing? What if we could create artificial brains that could solve problems that are currently beyond the reach of traditional computers? This is the promise of **organoid intelligence (OI)**, a new and rapidly developing field that is poised to revolutionise the way we think about computing.

OI is based on the idea of using **brain organoids**, which are tiny, three-dimensional structures grown from human stem cells, to create biological computers. Scientists are making remarkable progress in creating increasingly complex and functional brain organoids in the lab. These organoids, essentially "brains in a dish," offer an unprecedented opportunity to study the human brain and develop new treatments for neurological disorders. But they also hold the potential to be used as powerful computational devices.

The potential of OI is vast. It could be used to:

- **Develop new drugs and therapies for diseases like Alzheimer's and Parkinson's.** Imagine being able to test the effectiveness of new drugs on brain organoids that are genetically identical to the patient, allowing for truly personalised medicine.
- **Create new types of biocomputers that can solve complex problems that are difficult or impossible for traditional computers.** Imagine biocomputers that can learn and adapt like the human brain, potentially unlocking solutions to some of humanity's greatest challenges.
- **Enhance our understanding of the human brain and consciousness.** Imagine the insights we could gain into the workings of the mind by studying these miniature, living models of our own brains.

However, OI also raises a number of ethical concerns.

- **Is it morally acceptable to create and use brain organoids for research?** These organoids, while not fully developed brains, do possess some of the functional characteristics of the human brain, raising questions about their potential for sentience and the ethical implications of using them for experimentation.
- **Could OI systems become so intelligent that they pose a threat to humanity?** As

we push the boundaries of OI, it's essential to consider the potential risks of creating artificial intelligence that could surpass human capabilities.

- **How can we ensure that OI is used for good and not for harm?** As with any powerful technology, OI has the potential to be misused. It's crucial that we develop ethical guidelines and regulations to ensure that it is used responsibly.

The development of OI is still in its early stages. But the potential of this technology is enormous. OI has the potential to revolutionise computing, medicine, and our understanding of the human brain. However, it is important to proceed with caution and to address the ethical concerns that are raised by this technology. The future of OI is uncertain, but one thing is clear: **this is a technology that has the potential to change the world.**

CHAPTER 1

The Astonishing Capabilities of the Human Brain

The human brain is the most complex structure in the known universe. It is a biological marvel, containing billions of neurons interconnected in intricate networks that defy complete understanding, even with today's advanced technology. This intricate organ, weighing just over a kilogram, orchestrates every aspect of our being. It allows us to sense the world around us, experience a vast spectrum of emotions, learn and remember, and even ponder our own existence.

The brain's ability to process information is astounding. It can take in a constant stream of data from our senses, filter out the noise, and focus on what is important. It can make decisions in fractions of a second, often based on incomplete information, and learn from its mistakes. Our brains are the seat of our consciousness, the essence of who we are. They hold our memories, shape our personalities, and drive our creativity.

How Does the Brain Learn?

Learning is a fundamental process of the brain that allows us to adapt to our environment and acquire new skills and knowledge. The brain's capacity for learning is remarkable. From the moment we are born, our brains are constantly absorbing information, making connections, and refining existing ones.

One of the key mechanisms of learning is **synaptic plasticity**, the ability of the connections between neurons, called synapses, to strengthen or weaken over time. When we learn something new, the synapses involved in that learning process are strengthened, making it easier for those neurons to communicate with each other in the future. This strengthening of connections is what allows us to remember information and perform tasks more efficiently.

Memory: A Tapestry of Experiences

Memory is another crucial function of the brain, allowing us to store and retrieve information from past experiences. The brain doesn't store memories in a single location like a computer hard drive. Instead, memories are distributed across vast networks of neurons.

Different types of memories are stored in different parts of the brain. Short-term memories, such as remembering a phone number for a few seconds, are held in the **prefrontal cortex**. Long-term memories, such as childhood events or factual knowledge, are stored in the **hippocampus** and other areas of the brain.

The Power of Information Processing

The brain is constantly processing information, even when we are not consciously aware of it. It filters through the torrent of sensory input, making sense of the world around us. This processing happens at an incredible speed, allowing us to react to stimuli, make decisions, and carry out complex actions in real-time.

The brain's ability to process information is not only fast but also highly adaptable. It can adjust to changing circumstances, learn new patterns, and find creative solutions to problems. This adaptability is what makes us such versatile and resilient creatures.

Unlocking the Mysteries of the Brain

Despite the immense progress in neuroscience, much about the brain remains a mystery. How consciousness arises from the complex interplay of neurons is still largely unknown. The intricate workings of memory, emotion, and creativity are still being unravelled.

Understanding the brain's complexity is one of the grand challenges facing science. It is a quest that holds immense promise, not only for understanding ourselves but also for developing new technologies that can enhance human capabilities and address neurological disorders that affect millions worldwide.

CHAPTER 2

The Limitations of Traditional Computing

The human brain, with its unparalleled complexity and adaptability, sets a high bar for artificial intelligence. While traditional computing has made remarkable strides in recent decades, it still pales in comparison to the brain's remarkable capabilities. Traditional computers, based on silicon chips and digital logic, are excellent at performing repetitive calculations at high speed. They excel in tasks like data processing, number crunching, and running complex algorithms. However, they struggle with tasks that humans find relatively easy, such as recognizing faces, understanding natural language, and adapting to new situations.

The Constraints of Silicon

Traditional computers rely on a fundamentally different architecture than the human brain. They process information sequentially, executing one instruction at a time. This linear approach can be highly efficient for well-defined tasks with clear rules. However, it becomes a bottleneck when dealing with the complexities of the real world, where information is often ambiguous, incomplete, and constantly changing.

Energy Consumption: A Growing Concern

Another significant limitation of traditional computing is its energy consumption. As computers become more powerful, they require increasingly more energy to operate. This poses a challenge for both sustainability and scalability. The human brain, in contrast, is incredibly energy-efficient. It performs its remarkable feats of information processing while consuming only about 20 watts of power, roughly the same as a dim light bulb.

Moore's Law and Its Limits

For decades, the computing industry has relied on Moore's Law, which states that the number of transistors that can be placed on an integrated circuit doubles approximately every two years. This exponential growth in processing power has driven the digital revolution. However, Moore's Law is approaching its physical limits. As transistors shrink to the size of just a few atoms, quantum effects start to interfere with their operation, making further miniaturization increasingly difficult and expensive.

The Rise of Artificial Intelligence

Artificial intelligence (AI) has emerged as a powerful tool for solving complex problems. AI algorithms can learn from data, identify patterns, and make predictions with remarkable accuracy. However, even the most advanced AI systems still fall short of human-level intelligence in many areas. AI often struggles with tasks that require common sense, intuition, and the ability to understand context.

The Need for a New Paradigm

The limitations of traditional computing and the challenges faced by AI highlight the need for a new paradigm in computing. A paradigm that can mimic the brain's efficiency, adaptability, and capacity for learning. This is where the concept of biocomputing, and in particular, organoid intelligence (OI), comes into play. OI offers the potential to bridge the gap between the digital world of computers and the biological world of the human brain, opening up exciting new possibilities for the future of computing.

CHAPTER 3

Biocomputing: A New Frontier

As we've seen, traditional computing, while powerful, faces inherent limitations in its ability to truly mimic the human brain's capabilities. The search for alternatives has led to the exciting field of **biocomputing**, which seeks to harness biological systems for computation. This innovative approach draws inspiration from nature's elegant solutions, aiming to create computers that are more efficient, adaptable, and potentially even more intelligent than their silicon-based counterparts.

Biocomputing: Diverse Approaches

Biocomputing encompasses a wide range of approaches, each with its unique strengths and challenges. Some researchers are exploring the use of **DNA**, the molecule that carries genetic information, as a computational medium. DNA's remarkable capacity for information storage and its ability to perform complex molecular operations make it an attractive candidate for biocomputing.

Another promising avenue within biocomputing involves utilizing **molecules** and their interactions to perform computations. This approach leverages the principles of chemistry and physics to create molecular circuits and devices capable of carrying out logical operations.

Perhaps the most intriguing and ambitious branch of biocomputing focuses on utilizing **living cells** as computational units. This is where **organoid intelligence (OI)** comes into play. OI represents a revolutionary concept that aims to leverage the computational power of brain organoids, those "brains in a dish", to create a new generation of biological computers.

Organoid Intelligence: The Potential

OI holds immense promise for overcoming the limitations of traditional computing and pushing the boundaries of artificial intelligence. By harnessing the unique properties of brain organoids, OI could lead to computers that are:

- **More Energy-Efficient**: Brain organoids, like the human brain, are remarkably energy-efficient. They can perform complex computations while consuming a fraction of the energy required by traditional computers. This could lead to more sustainable computing solutions, reducing our reliance on energy-intensive data centres.
- **More Adaptable**: Brain organoids exhibit a degree of plasticity and adaptability that is difficult to replicate in traditional computing.

They can learn from experience, adjust to new information, and even rewire themselves to some extent. This adaptability could lead to computers that are more robust and resilient, capable of handling complex and unpredictable situations.

- **Capable of Higher-Level Cognition**: Brain organoids, though still in their early stages of development, possess the potential to exhibit higher-level cognitive functions, such as learning, memory, and even rudimentary decision-making. This opens up the tantalizing possibility of creating computers that can truly "think" and "reason" in ways that are currently beyond the reach of traditional AI.

The Dawn of a New Era?

The field of biocomputing, and OI in particular, is still in its infancy. There are significant technical challenges to overcome before these technologies can be fully realized. However, the potential benefits are so profound that research in this area is rapidly accelerating.

The development of OI could revolutionize not only computing but also medicine, neuroscience, and our understanding of the human brain. It could lead to new treatments for neurological disorders, personalized medicine tailored to individual patients, and even enhance human cognitive abilities.

However, as with any powerful technology, OI also raises ethical concerns that must be carefully considered. The potential for creating entities with a degree of sentience or consciousness, the implications for human autonomy, and the risks of misuse are just some of the issues that need to be addressed as this technology advances. The future of biocomputing, and of OI, is full of promise and potential pitfalls. It is a journey that requires careful navigation, balancing the pursuit of scientific progress with a deep understanding of its ethical implications. The choices we make today will shape the future of this transformative technology and its impact on humanity.

CHAPTER 4

*Understanding Organoids: Building
Blocks of Biocomputing*

Organoids represent a groundbreaking advancement in biological research, offering a fascinating window into the complexities of human organs and their development. These three-dimensional structures, grown from stem cells in a laboratory setting, mimic the structure and function of organs in the human body with remarkable accuracy. While organoids have been created for various organs, including the liver, kidneys, and intestines, brain organoids hold particular significance for the field of biocomputing and organoid intelligence (OI).

Stem Cells: The Seeds of Organoids

The creation of organoids begins with **stem cells**, the body's master cells capable of differentiating into various cell types. Stem cells can be derived from different sources, including embryonic stem cells, induced pluripotent stem cells (iPSCs), and adult stem cells. Each type of stem cell has its own unique characteristics and potential applications.

Growing Organoids in the Lab

The process of growing organoids is a testament to the ingenuity of scientists and their understanding of developmental biology. Stem cells are carefully cultured in a controlled environment that mimics the conditions within the human body. They are provided with a specific cocktail of nutrients, growth factors, and scaffolding materials that guide their differentiation and self-organisation into three-dimensional structures resembling miniature organs.

Brain Organoids: A Window into the Brain

Brain organoids, also known as "mini-brains," are particularly fascinating. These tiny structures, typically just a few millimetres in diameter, exhibit some of the key features of the human brain, including distinct regions like the cortex, hippocampus, and even rudimentary neural networks. While brain organoids are far from being fully functional replicas of the human brain, they provide an invaluable tool for studying brain development, disease modelling, and drug discovery.

The Potential of Organoids

Organoids have already made significant contributions to our understanding of human biology and disease. They offer a powerful platform for:

- **Disease Modelling**: Organoids can be used to model a wide range of diseases, including genetic disorders, infectious diseases, and even cancer. By studying how diseases manifest in organoids, researchers can gain insights into the underlying mechanisms and develop more effective treatments.

- **Drug Discovery**: Organoids provide a more accurate and human-relevant model for testing the efficacy and safety of new drugs. Traditional drug screening methods often rely on animal models or cell cultures, which may not fully capture the complexities of human biology. Organoids offer a more predictive system for evaluating potential drug candidates, potentially reducing the time and cost of drug development.

- **Personalized Medicine**: The future of medicine lies in personalized treatments tailored to an individual's unique genetic makeup and disease characteristics. Organoids derived from a patient's own cells hold the potential to revolutionize personalized medicine. These "patient-specific" organoids could be used to test the effectiveness of different treatment options, identify potential drug sensitivities or resistances, and guide clinical decision-making.

Brain Organoids and Biocomputing

Brain organoids, with their potential to exhibit some level of cognitive function, are particularly intriguing for biocomputing. While still in its early stages, OI research aims to harness the computational power of these mini-brains to create a new generation of biological computers.

The development of OI faces significant technical hurdles. Scientists are working on developing methods to:

- **Scale Up Organoid Production**: Creating large numbers of brain organoids with consistent quality and functionality is crucial for advancing OI research.
- **Enhance Organoid Complexity**: Current brain organoids are relatively simple compared to the human brain. Researchers are exploring ways to create more complex and sophisticated organoids that better mimic the intricate structure and function of the brain.
- **Develop Effective Interfaces**: Communicating with brain organoids and interpreting their signals is essential for utilizing their computational power. Scientists are developing advanced brain-computer interfaces that can record and stimulate neural activity in organoids.

Ethical Considerations

As with any powerful technology, organoid research, particularly in the context of OI, raises ethical considerations that must be carefully addressed.

- **Sentience and Consciousness**: As brain organoids become more complex, the question of whether they could develop a degree of sentience or consciousness needs to be addressed. Clear ethical guidelines and regulations are needed to ensure that organoids are treated with appropriate respect and care.

- **Donor Consent and Privacy**: Organoids derived from patient cells raise issues of donor consent and privacy. It is crucial to establish clear protocols for obtaining informed consent from donors and safeguarding their genetic information.

The Future of Organoids

Organoids represent a remarkable scientific achievement with the potential to transform medicine, neuroscience, and even computing. As research progresses and ethical considerations are carefully addressed, organoids hold the promise of unlocking new frontiers in our understanding of human biology and ushering in a new era of biocomputing.

CHAPTER 5

Constructing Brains in a Dish: The
Genesis of Brain Organoids

The creation of brain organoids, often referred to as "mini-brains," represents a remarkable feat of bioengineering. These tiny, self-organising structures, grown from stem cells in a laboratory setting, offer a glimpse into the intricate processes that govern brain development and hold immense potential for advancing our understanding of the brain, treating neurological disorders, and potentially even revolutionising computing.

From Stem Cells to Three-Dimensional Brains

The journey of a brain organoid begins with stem cells, the versatile building blocks of the human body. Scientists typically use either pluripotent stem cells, which have the ability to differentiate into any cell type in the body, or neural progenitor cells, which are already committed to becoming brain cells.

These stem cells are carefully nurtured in a controlled laboratory environment that mimics the conditions within the developing human brain. They are immersed in a nutrient-rich medium and provided with a precise cocktail of growth factors, signalling molecules that guide their differentiation and self-organisation.

As the stem cells multiply and differentiate, they begin to form three-dimensional structures that resemble the early stages of brain development. They spontaneously arrange themselves into distinct layers, reminiscent of the cortex, the outermost layer of the brain responsible for higher cognitive functions. Within these layers, different types of brain cells emerge, including neurons, the information-processing cells of the brain, and glial cells, which provide support and insulation for neurons.

Mimicking Nature's Blueprint

What is truly remarkable about brain organoids is their ability to self-organise, following a developmental program encoded within their DNA. Scientists provide the basic building blocks and environmental cues, but it is the intrinsic properties of the stem cells themselves that drive their transformation into complex, three-dimensional structures resembling the brain.

This self-organising capacity of brain organoids highlights a fundamental principle of developmental biology: the blueprint for building a brain is not a rigid set of instructions but rather a dynamic process of self-assembly guided by local interactions between cells and their environment.

Challenges in Organoid Development

While the creation of brain organoids represents a significant scientific breakthrough, several challenges remain.

- **Vascularisation**: One of the key limitations of current brain organoids is the lack of a functional vascular system, the network of blood vessels that supply oxygen and nutrients to the brain. Without a vascular system, organoids can only grow to a certain size before the cells in the core begin to starve. Researchers are exploring innovative techniques, such as incorporating endothelial cells, the cells that line blood vessels, into organoids or developing artificial scaffolds that promote vascularisation.

- **Maturation**: Brain organoids, while structurally similar to the developing human brain, often exhibit a level of maturity equivalent to that of a foetus. They lack the complex interconnectivity and functional sophistication of the adult human brain. Scientists are investigating ways to promote further maturation of organoids, such as exposing them to electrical stimulation or transplanting them into animal models.

- **Reproducibility**: Creating brain organoids with consistent size, structure, and functionality is crucial for research and potential applications. Variability between organoids can arise from differences in stem cell sources, culture conditions, and other experimental factors. Standardising protocols and developing more robust culture systems are essential for ensuring reproducibility.

Scaling Up Production

Another challenge in organoid research is scaling up production. Currently, creating large numbers of brain organoids for research or potential applications is a time-consuming and labour-intensive process. Automating organoid production and developing more efficient culture systems are crucial for making these technologies more widely accessible.

The Future of Brain Organoids

Despite these challenges, the future of brain organoids is bright. As researchers continue to refine techniques and overcome limitations, brain organoids hold immense potential for:

- **Unraveling the Mysteries of Brain Development**: Brain organoids provide an unprecedented opportunity to study the intricate processes that govern brain development. By observing how stem cells differentiate, migrate, and connect to form complex neural networks, scientists can gain insights into the fundamental mechanisms underlying brain formation.
- **Modeling Neurological Disorders**: Brain organoids derived from patients with

neurological disorders, such as Alzheimer's disease, Parkinson's disease, and autism spectrum disorder, offer a powerful tool for studying the cellular and molecular basis of these conditions. These "disease-in-a-dish" models can help researchers identify potential drug targets and develop more effective therapies.

- **Revolutionising Drug Discovery**: Brain organoids provide a more accurate and human-relevant model for testing the efficacy and safety of new drugs for neurological disorders. Traditional drug screening methods often rely on animal models, which may not fully capture the complexities of the human brain. Organoids offer a more predictive system for evaluating potential drug candidates, potentially accelerating the drug development process.

- **Advancing Personalised Medicine**: Organoids derived from a patient's own cells hold the potential to revolutionise personalised medicine. These "patient-specific" organoids could be used to test the effectiveness of different treatment options, predict drug responses, and guide clinical decision-making.

- **Paving the Way for Organoid Intelligence**: The most ambitious application of brain organoids lies in the field of organoid intelligence (OI). Researchers envision using brain organoids as biological computers, harnessing their inherent computational power to solve complex problems, model human cognition, and potentially even enhance human intelligence.

The creation of brain organoids represents a remarkable convergence of biology, engineering, and computer science. These tiny, self-organising structures offer a window into the complexities of the human brain and hold immense potential for advancing our understanding of this most enigmatic organ, developing new therapies for neurological disorders, and potentially even shaping the future of computing.

CHAPTER 6

The Ethical Labyrinth: Navigating the
Moral Dimensions of Brain Organoids

The rapid advancement of brain organoid technology has opened up a Pandora's box of ethical questions, challenging our understanding of consciousness, sentience, and the very definition of what it means to be human. As we venture further into this uncharted territory, it is imperative to engage in a thoughtful and nuanced discussion about the moral implications of creating and using these "mini-brains."

The Spectre of Sentience

Perhaps the most pressing ethical concern surrounding brain organoids is the potential for sentience. Could these tiny structures, mimicking the architecture and function of the human brain, develop the capacity for subjective experience, awareness, and feelings? While current brain organoids are far from exhibiting anything resembling human consciousness, the rapid pace of progress raises the possibility that future generations of organoids, with increased complexity and functionality, could cross this threshold.

The emergence of sentience in brain organoids would have profound ethical implications. It would demand a reassessment of their moral status, potentially granting them rights and protections similar to those afforded to humans or other sentient beings. It would also raise questions about the permissibility of using sentient organoids for research, particularly if it involves procedures that could cause them pain or distress.

Blurring the Lines of Identity

Brain organoids derived from a patient's own cells raise unique ethical considerations related to personal identity and privacy. These "personalised" organoids, carrying the genetic blueprint of an individual, could potentially be used to model their cognitive abilities, predict their susceptibility to neurological disorders, or even test the effects of drugs on their brain.

The use of patient-derived organoids raises concerns about the potential for misuse or exploitation of this highly personal information. It also begs the question of whether an individual has a right to control the use of their own cells, even after they have been transformed into an organoid.

Navigating Informed Consent

Obtaining informed consent for the use of cells to create brain organoids presents a complex ethical challenge. Donors typically provide consent for the use of their cells in general research, but they may not fully comprehend the implications of their cells being used to create brain organoids, especially given the rapidly evolving nature of this field.

Ensuring that donors are adequately informed about the potential risks, benefits, and ethical considerations associated with brain organoid research is paramount. This includes providing clear and accessible information about the possibility of organoid sentience, the potential for personalised applications, and the implications for privacy and identity.

Intellectual Property and Accessibility

The development of brain organoid technology raises complex questions about intellectual property rights. Who owns the rights to these "mini-brains"? Is it the researchers who created them, the donors whose cells were used, or society as a whole?

The issue of intellectual property rights has implications for the accessibility and affordability of brain organoid technology. If patents restrict access to this technology, it could limit its potential benefits for research, drug development, and clinical applications.

Balancing Progress with Responsibility

The ethical considerations surrounding brain organoids highlight the need for responsible innovation in this rapidly evolving field. Scientists, ethicists, policymakers, and the public must engage in an ongoing dialogue to establish guidelines and regulations that ensure the ethical development and use of brain organoid technology.

This dialogue should address key questions such as:

- What level of sentience, if any, would warrant moral consideration for brain organoids?
- How can we ensure that informed consent procedures adequately address the unique ethical considerations of brain organoid research?
- How can we balance intellectual property rights with the need to make this technology accessible for the benefit of society?
- What mechanisms can we put in place to monitor and regulate the development and use of brain organoids?

Charting a Course for the Future

The creation of brain organoids represents a profound scientific achievement, offering unprecedented opportunities to understand the human brain, develop new therapies for neurological disorders, and potentially even revolutionise computing. However, this technology also raises profound ethical questions that demand careful consideration and responsible stewardship.

As we venture further into this uncharted territory, it is imperative to remember that scientific progress must be guided by ethical principles. By engaging in open and transparent discussions about the moral dimensions of brain organoid technology, we can chart a course for the future that balances the pursuit of knowledge with the protection of human dignity and the promotion of human well-being.

CHAPTER 7

Organoid Intelligence: A New Dawn in Biocomputing

Organoid intelligence (OI) represents a radical departure from traditional computing and artificial intelligence, promising a future where biological systems become the architects of complex problem-solving. By harnessing the remarkable computational power of brain organoids, scientists are on the cusp of unlocking a new era of biocomputing with potentially transformative applications across diverse fields.

Organoid Intelligence: The Basics

At its core, organoid intelligence seeks to harness the computational capabilities of brain organoids, essentially "thinking" structures grown in a laboratory. These three-dimensional cultures of brain cells, derived from stem cells, self-organise into complex networks that mimic the architecture and functionality of the human brain, albeit on a much smaller scale.

While current brain organoids are far from achieving the sophistication of the human brain, they exhibit rudimentary cognitive abilities, such as learning, memory, and basic information processing. Scientists believe that by carefully nurturing and stimulating these organoids, they can be coaxed into developing more complex cognitive functions, paving the way for a new generation of biocomputers.

The Allure of Organoid Intelligence

Organoid intelligence holds several potential advantages over traditional computing and artificial intelligence, particularly in areas where these technologies struggle:

- **Energy Efficiency:** Biological systems are remarkably energy-efficient, performing complex computations with a fraction of the energy consumed by silicon-based computers. Organoid-based biocomputers could potentially revolutionise energy consumption in computing, leading to more sustainable and environmentally friendly technologies.
- **Parallel Processing:** The human brain excels at parallel processing, handling multiple streams of information simultaneously. Organoid intelligence could leverage this inherent capability of biological systems to develop highly efficient parallel processing architectures, surpassing the limitations of current computing models.
- **Learning and Adaptation:** Brain organoids possess an inherent capacity for learning and adaptation, constantly rewiring their neural

connections in response to new information and experiences. This inherent plasticity could enable organoid-based biocomputers to learn and adapt to complex and dynamic environments, surpassing the capabilities of traditional AI systems that often struggle with adaptability.

- **Biological Insight:** Organoid intelligence offers a unique window into the inner workings of the human brain, potentially leading to breakthroughs in our understanding of consciousness, cognition, and neurological disorders. By studying how organoids learn and process information, scientists could gain unprecedented insights into the fundamental principles of biological intelligence.

Key Research Trajectories in Organoid Intelligence

The field of organoid intelligence is still in its nascent stages, but several key research trajectories are rapidly gaining momentum:

- **Enhancing Organoid Complexity:** Scientists are constantly refining techniques to grow larger, more complex, and more functional brain organoids. By introducing new cell types, manipulating the organoid's environment, and using bioengineering approaches, researchers aim to create organoids that more closely resemble the intricate architecture and functionality of the human brain.

- **Developing Biocompatible Interfaces:** A major challenge in organoid intelligence lies in establishing effective communication channels between biological and silicon-based systems. Researchers are developing sophisticated brain-computer interfaces, using microelectrode arrays, implantable probes, and even optical techniques to record and interpret signals from organoids, bridging the gap between the biological and digital realms.

- **Training Organoids for Specific Tasks:** Scientists are exploring various methods to teach organoids to perform basic computational tasks, such as pattern recognition, image classification, and even simple decision-making. By carefully controlling the organoid's environment, providing targeted stimulation, and using reinforcement learning algorithms, researchers aim to train organoids to perform increasingly complex tasks.

The Dawn of a New Era

Organoid intelligence is poised to revolutionise our understanding of the brain and unlock unprecedented computational capabilities. As this field matures, it has the potential to reshape industries, accelerate scientific discovery, and fundamentally alter our relationship with technology. However, the development and application of organoid intelligence must be guided by ethical considerations, ensuring that this powerful technology is used responsibly for the benefit of humanity.

CHAPTER 8

Bridging Worlds: Interfacing with
Organoid Intelligence

One of the most significant hurdles in the burgeoning field of organoid intelligence (OI) lies in establishing a reliable and effective means of communication between these biological "mini-brains" and the digital world. Scientists are actively exploring a range of innovative techniques to bridge this gap, developing sophisticated brain-computer interfaces (BCIs) that can both record the subtle electrical whispers of organoid activity and translate those signals into meaningful data.

Deciphering the Organoid's Language

Brain organoids, while rudimentary in their current form, exhibit a symphony of electrical activity, a chorus of neuronal chatter that reflects their internal processing and responses to external stimuli. To tap into this intricate language, scientists are employing a variety of techniques, each with its own strengths and limitations:

- **Microelectrode Arrays (MEAs):** These postage stamp-sized grids of tiny electrodes provide a non-invasive way to listen in on the electrical activity of an entire organoid. Placed beneath the organoid, the MEA acts like a sensitive microphone, picking up the collective electrical hum of thousands of neurons firing in concert. This technique offers a broad overview of the organoid's activity, but it lacks the precision to isolate individual neurons or specific neural pathways.

- **Implantable Probes:** For a more targeted approach, scientists are developing miniature probes that can be gently inserted into the organoid, allowing researchers to eavesdrop on the conversations of specific groups of neurons. These probes, often equipped with multiple recording sites, can capture the nuanced electrical signals of individual neurons or small clusters, providing a more detailed view of the organoid's inner workings. However, the invasive nature of these probes poses challenges, potentially disrupting the organoid's delicate structure and limiting long-term recordings.

- **Optical Imaging:** Emerging optical techniques offer a glimpse into the organoid's activity without the need for physical contact. By engineering organoids to express fluorescent proteins that light up when neurons fire, scientists can visualise the patterns of activity across the entire organoid. This approach provides a non-invasive and visually compelling way to observe the organoid's response to stimuli, but it currently lacks the temporal resolution to capture the rapid-fire electrical signals of individual neurons.

From Electrical Whispers to Meaningful Data

Interpreting the raw data collected from these BCIs poses another significant challenge. The electrical signals emanating from an organoid, while rich with information, are often subtle, noisy, and complex. Scientists are developing sophisticated algorithms and machine learning techniques to sift through this data, identifying patterns and extracting meaningful insights:

- **Spike Detection and Sorting:** One of the first steps in analysing organoid data involves identifying individual "spikes" – the characteristic electrical signatures of neurons firing. This process, known as spike sorting, uses algorithms to tease apart the overlapping signals from multiple neurons recorded simultaneously, allowing researchers to isolate the activity of specific cells.
- **Network Analysis:** By analysing the patterns of spikes across multiple neurons, scientists can begin to understand the functional connections within the organoid, mapping out the intricate web of neural pathways that underlie its activity. This network analysis

can reveal how information flows through the organoid, identifying hubs of activity and key pathways involved in specific tasks or responses.

- **Decoding Organoid Output:** A crucial goal in OI research is to develop methods for decoding the organoid's "output" – the patterns of activity that represent its response to a particular stimulus or its attempt to perform a specific task. Scientists are exploring various approaches, including machine learning algorithms trained to recognise specific patterns of activity associated with different outputs, allowing them to interpret the organoid's response in a meaningful way.

Challenges and Opportunities on the Horizon

Despite significant progress, interfacing with organoid intelligence remains a challenging endeavour, fraught with technical and conceptual hurdles. The signals from organoids are often faint and prone to interference, requiring highly sensitive recording equipment and sophisticated signal processing techniques. Moreover, the complexity of organoid activity, with its intricate interplay of thousands of neurons, makes it difficult to isolate specific signals and interpret their meaning.

However, the rapid pace of innovation in BCI technology and data analysis offers exciting opportunities for the future. Advances in microfabrication are leading to smaller, more flexible, and biocompatible probes that can be seamlessly integrated with organoids, enabling long-term, high-resolution recordings. Meanwhile, the development of powerful machine learning algorithms is accelerating our ability to decipher the complex language of organoid activity, extracting meaningful insights from the sea of data.

As we refine our ability to communicate with organoid intelligence, we open the door to a world of possibilities. Imagine a future where organoid-based biocomputers, seamlessly integrated with digital systems, augment our own cognitive abilities, accelerate scientific discovery, and even contribute to the development of new forms of artificial intelligence that more closely resemble the remarkable adaptability and learning capacity of the human brain.

CHAPTER 9

Sculpting Minds: The Art and Science of Organoid Learning

Scientists are embarking on a journey that echoes the ancient craft of sculpting, not with chisel and stone, but with carefully orchestrated stimuli and feedback loops. Their medium? The burgeoning field of organoid intelligence. The goal? To guide brain organoids towards learning, shaping their neural networks to perform tasks and potentially unlock higher cognitive abilities. This chapter explores the fascinating and challenging endeavour of making organoids learn.

The Building Blocks of Learning

Organoid learning, in essence, mirrors the fundamental principles of learning in any biological system. It hinges on the brain's remarkable plasticity – the ability of neural networks to rewire themselves in response to experiences. This rewiring process, driven by changes in the strength and connections between neurons, underpins the formation of memories, the acquisition of skills, and the development of cognitive abilities.

To guide organoid learning, scientists draw upon a

toolbox of techniques inspired by neuroscience and machine learning:

- **Stimulation:** Just as our brains thrive on a rich tapestry of sensory input, organoids need stimulation to learn and grow. This stimulation can take various forms, from electrical pulses delivered via microelectrode arrays to carefully crafted patterns of light projected onto light-sensitive cells within the organoid. The type, intensity, and timing of stimulation play a crucial role in shaping the organoid's neural activity and driving learning.
- **Feedback:** Learning is an iterative process that relies on feedback to guide progress. Organoids, like any learner, need to know whether their responses are correct or incorrect, and how to adjust their behaviour accordingly. This feedback can be provided through various mechanisms, such as rewarding correct responses with a burst of electrical stimulation or penalising incorrect responses with a brief period of silence.
- **Reinforcement Learning:** A powerful paradigm borrowed from machine learning, reinforcement learning has emerged as a promising approach to training organoids. In this approach, the organoid is presented with a task and receives rewards for performing the task correctly. Over time, the organoid learns

to associate specific actions with positive outcomes, gradually optimising its behaviour to maximise rewards.

The Current Landscape of Organoid Learning

While still in its infancy, the field of organoid learning has already yielded intriguing results, demonstrating the feasibility of teaching organoids to perform basic tasks:

- **Pattern Recognition:** Researchers have successfully trained organoids to recognise simple visual patterns, such as horizontal and vertical lines. By presenting the organoids with repeated examples of these patterns and providing feedback on their responses, scientists have observed the emergence of specialised neural circuits dedicated to pattern recognition within the organoid.
- **Spatial Navigation:** In a virtual environment, organoids have shown the ability to learn simple spatial navigation tasks, such as finding their way through a maze. By providing the organoid with virtual sensory inputs mimicking the experience of moving through the maze and rewarding it for reaching the goal, scientists have witnessed the organoid developing rudimentary spatial awareness.
- **Decision-Making:** Organoids have even demonstrated the capacity for simple decision-

making, choosing between different options based on the potential rewards associated with each choice. By carefully manipulating the reward structure of the task, researchers have observed the organoid gradually learning to make decisions that maximise its chances of receiving a reward.

Challenges and Future Directions

While the early successes in organoid learning are promising, the field faces significant challenges:

- **Scaling Complexity:** Current brain organoids, while impressive in their own right, are still relatively simple compared to the human brain. Scaling up the complexity of organoids, both in terms of cell diversity and the number of neurons, is a major hurdle that needs to be overcome to unlock higher cognitive abilities.

- **Decoding Neural Activity:** Interpreting the vast and intricate patterns of neural activity within an organoid remains a formidable challenge. Developing sophisticated techniques to decode these signals and understand the organoid's internal representations of information is crucial for effectively training and communicating with organoids.

- **Ethical Considerations:** As organoids become more sophisticated and potentially capable of more complex cognitive feats, the ethical implications of organoid learning come to the forefront. Questions about the potential for sentience, consciousness, and the moral status of organoids demand careful consideration and ongoing dialogue between scientists, ethicists, and society as a whole.

Unlocking the Potential of Organoid Intelligence

The journey of making organoids learn is fraught with challenges, but the potential rewards are immense. By unlocking the secrets of organoid learning, we could not only gain unprecedented insights into the workings of the human brain but also pave the way for a new generation of biocomputers capable of solving complex problems that elude traditional computing approaches.

The future of organoid intelligence hinges on our ability to nurture and guide the learning process, shaping these tiny minds into powerful tools for scientific discovery, technological innovation, and perhaps even a deeper understanding of ourselves.

CHAPTER 10

Organoid Intelligence: A New Frontier in
Drug Discovery and Disease Modelling

Organoid intelligence (OI) is poised to revolutionise the way we develop drugs and study diseases, particularly those affecting the brain. By providing a more accurate and human-relevant model of brain function, OI offers unprecedented opportunities to accelerate drug discovery, personalise treatments, and gain deeper insights into the complexities of neurological disorders.

Accelerated Drug Discovery with Human Relevance

Traditional drug development relies heavily on animal models and cell cultures, which often fail to accurately predict drug efficacy and safety in humans. The intricate architecture and cellular diversity of the human brain are simply too complex to replicate in these simplified models.

Organoid intelligence offers a promising alternative, providing a more human-relevant platform for drug screening and testing. Brain organoids, with their three-dimensional structure and complex neural networks, more closely resemble the cellular and functional intricacies of the human brain, offering a more predictive model for drug responses.

Personalised Treatments: Organoid Avatars for Precision Medicine

Imagine a future where treatments for neurological disorders are tailored to the unique genetic and cellular makeup of each patient. OI has the potential to make this vision a reality by creating personalised "organoid avatars" - brain organoids derived from a patient's own cells.

These avatars would capture the specific genetic and cellular characteristics of the patient's disease, providing a powerful tool for predicting drug responses and identifying the most effective treatment strategies. By testing different drugs on a patient's organoid avatar, clinicians could identify the most effective treatment with minimal side effects, paving the way for truly personalised medicine.

Unravelling the Mysteries of Neurological Disorders

Neurological disorders, such as Alzheimer's disease, Parkinson's disease, and autism, pose significant challenges to scientists and clinicians alike. Their complex interplay of genetic and environmental factors, coupled with the intricate workings of the brain, makes it difficult to understand their underlying mechanisms and develop effective treatments.

OI offers a powerful new tool for studying these disorders, providing a human-relevant model system that captures the complexity of the human brain. Scientists can use brain organoids to investigate the cellular and molecular mechanisms of these diseases, identify potential drug targets, and test the efficacy of new therapies.

Disease Modelling in a Dish: Recreating Disease Pathology

OI enables scientists to recreate the pathology of neurological disorders in a dish, providing a controlled environment to study the disease process in detail. By introducing genetic mutations or environmental factors associated with a particular disorder, researchers can observe how these alterations affect the development and function of brain organoids.

This approach allows scientists to pinpoint the cellular and molecular events that drive disease progression, identify potential therapeutic targets, and test the efficacy of new drugs in a human-relevant model system.

Ethical Considerations: Navigating the Moral Landscape

The use of OI in drug discovery and disease modelling raises important ethical considerations, particularly as these organoids become more complex and sophisticated. Questions surrounding the potential for sentience, consciousness, and the moral status of organoids require careful consideration and open discussion.

Striking a balance between scientific progress and ethical responsibility is paramount in this emerging field. Open dialogue, transparent research practices, and robust ethical guidelines are essential to ensure that OI is used responsibly for the benefit of humanity.

The Promise of OI: A New Era in Medicine

Organoid intelligence holds immense promise for revolutionising drug discovery and disease modelling, ushering in a new era of personalised medicine and deeper understanding of neurological disorders. By harnessing the power of OI, we can accelerate the development of new therapies, improve treatment outcomes, and ultimately alleviate the suffering caused by these debilitating diseases. However, it is crucial to proceed with caution, ensuring that ethical considerations guide our exploration of this powerful technology.

CHAPTER 11

Organoid Intelligence for Personalised Medicine: Tailoring Treatments to the Individual

The prospect of personalised medicine, where treatments are precisely tailored to an individual's unique genetic and biological makeup, has long tantalized the medical community. Organoid intelligence (OI) offers a powerful new tool to realise this vision, particularly for neurological disorders that have traditionally proven challenging to treat effectively. This chapter explores the potential of OI for personalised medicine, examining how it could revolutionise the way we diagnose, treat, and manage these complex conditions.

Organoid Avatars: Mirroring the Patient's Biology

Imagine a future where every patient with a neurological disorder has a personalised "organoid avatar" – a miniature replica of their own brain grown in a laboratory. This avatar, created from the patient's own cells, would capture the unique genetic and cellular characteristics of their condition, providing an unprecedented level of detail and accuracy for personalised treatment planning.

By testing different drugs or treatment strategies on the patient's organoid avatar, clinicians could predict the individual's response with remarkable precision. This approach could help identify the most effective treatment with the fewest side effects, minimising the trial-and-error approach that often characterises current treatment strategies.

Predicting Drug Responses: Minimising Trial and Error

One of the most significant challenges in treating neurological disorders is the variability in patient responses to medication. What works well for one person might be ineffective or even harmful for another. This variability stems from a complex interplay of genetic factors, environmental influences, and the unique characteristics of the individual's disease.

OI offers a way to navigate this complexity by providing a personalised model for drug testing. By exposing a patient's organoid avatar to different medications, clinicians could observe how the organoid responds, predicting the patient's likely response with much greater accuracy than traditional methods. This could dramatically reduce the time and cost of finding the right treatment, while minimising the risk of adverse reactions.

Identifying Optimal Drug Combinations: A Symphony of Therapies

Many neurological disorders require a combination of medications to effectively manage symptoms and slow disease progression. Finding the optimal combination for each patient can be a daunting task, often involving a lengthy process of trial and error.

OI could streamline this process by allowing clinicians to test different drug combinations on a patient's organoid avatar. This would allow them to observe how the organoid responds to the combined effects of the medications, identifying the most effective combination with the fewest side effects. This approach could revolutionise the way we approach combination therapy, moving away from a one-size-fits-all approach to a truly personalised strategy.

Unveiling Individualised Disease Mechanisms: Tailoring Treatments to the Root Cause

Beyond simply predicting drug responses, OI could also help us understand the underlying mechanisms of disease in individual patients. By studying the cellular and molecular changes within a patient's organoid avatar, researchers could gain insights into the unique drivers of their condition.

This deeper understanding could lead to the development of highly targeted therapies that address the root cause of the disease in each individual. For example, if an organoid avatar reveals a specific genetic mutation driving the disease, researchers could develop gene therapies tailored to correct that mutation.

Monitoring Disease Progression: A Window into the Brain

OI could also provide a powerful tool for monitoring disease progression in individual patients. By regularly analysing the patient's organoid avatar, clinicians could track changes in the organoid's structure and function, reflecting the progression of the disease in the patient's brain. This real-time monitoring could help clinicians adjust treatment strategies as needed, ensuring the patient receives the most effective care throughout the course of their illness.

Challenges and Future Directions: Bridging the Gap Between Research and Reality

While the potential of OI for personalised medicine is immense, several challenges remain before this technology can be fully realised.

- **Scaling Up Organoid Production:** Creating personalised organoid avatars for every patient requires a significant increase in the efficiency and scalability of organoid production. Advances in automated organoid culture systems and bioprinting technologies are crucial to overcoming this hurdle.
- **Improving Organoid Complexity:** While

current brain organoids are remarkably sophisticated, they still lack the full complexity of the human brain. Further research is needed to improve the diversity of cell types within organoids and enhance their ability to model the intricate interactions between different brain regions.

- **Validating Organoid Models:** Rigorous validation of organoid models is essential to ensure they accurately reflect the patient's biology and predict their response to treatments. This requires extensive testing and comparison with clinical data from real patients.

Ethical Considerations: Navigating Uncharted Territory

As OI technology advances, it is crucial to address the ethical considerations surrounding its use. Questions about patient privacy, data security, and the potential for genetic discrimination must be carefully considered. Open dialogue, transparent research practices, and robust ethical guidelines are essential to ensure that OI is used responsibly and equitably.

The Future of Personalised Medicine: Empowering Patients with Precision

OI has the potential to revolutionise the way we approach neurological disorders, ushering in an era of personalised medicine where treatments are precisely tailored to the individual. By harnessing the power of organoid avatars, we can empower patients with more precise diagnoses, more effective treatments, and a greater sense of control over their health. This journey will require continued research, collaboration, and a steadfast commitment to ethical considerations, but the potential rewards are immeasurable.

CHAPTER 12

Organoid Intelligence: A New Dawn for Biological Computing

Organoid intelligence (OI) stands at the cusp of revolutionising the very foundations of computing. Imagine computers that operate not on silicon chips but on the complex biological networks of brain organoids – living, learning systems capable of solving problems in ways that traditional computers struggle to grasp. This chapter explores the potential of OI to create a new paradigm of biological computing, one that harnesses the unique capabilities of living systems to tackle the challenges of the future.

Beyond the Limits of Silicon: A New Computing Paradigm

Traditional silicon-based computing, while incredibly powerful, faces inherent limitations. The miniaturisation of transistors, the building blocks of computers, is reaching its physical limits. Moreover, the energy demands of these systems are skyrocketing, raising concerns about sustainability and environmental impact. Perhaps most importantly, traditional computers struggle with tasks that come naturally to the human brain, such as pattern recognition, learning, and decision-making in complex environments.

Organoid intelligence offers a radical departure from traditional computing, promising a new paradigm that overcomes these limitations. By harnessing the computational power of living neural networks, OI could lead to the development of biocomputers with unprecedented capabilities:

- **Energy Efficiency:** Biological systems operate with remarkable energy efficiency, far surpassing that of silicon-based computers. OI could lead to the creation of ultra-low-power computers that consume significantly less energy, reducing our reliance on fossil fuels and mitigating environmental impact.
- **Parallel Processing:** The human brain excels at parallel processing, handling multiple streams of information simultaneously. OI could unlock the potential of massive parallel processing in biocomputers, enabling them to tackle complex problems that currently require vast amounts of time and computational resources.
- **Learning and Adaptation:** Traditional computers are programmed with fixed algorithms, limiting their ability to learn and adapt to new situations. OI, with its basis in living, learning systems, could lead to the development of biocomputers that

learn from experience, adapting to changing environments and evolving their capabilities over time.

Harnessing the Power of OI: Towards Practical Applications

The transition from laboratory curiosity to practical applications requires overcoming several challenges:

- **Scaling Up OI Systems:** Current brain organoids, while impressive, are still relatively small and simple compared to the human brain. Scaling up the size and complexity of these systems while maintaining their stability and functionality is a major hurdle.
- **Interfacing with OI:** Developing robust and reliable interfaces to communicate with OI systems is essential for both training and harnessing their computational power. Advances in brain-computer interfaces, such as microelectrode arrays and implantable probes, are paving the way for seamless communication between biological and artificial systems.
- **Understanding OI Computation:** Decoding the complex neural activity within an organoid and understanding how it represents and processes information is crucial for developing algorithms and architectures that can effectively utilise OI for computation. This requires a deep understanding of both

neuroscience and computer science.

A Future Shaped by OI: Opportunities and Challenges

The development of OI for biological computing has far-reaching implications, potentially transforming numerous fields:

- **Drug Discovery and Development:** OI-based biocomputers could simulate the effects of drugs on the human brain with unprecedented accuracy, accelerating drug development and reducing the reliance on animal models.
- **Material Science and Engineering:** OI systems could be used to design and discover new materials with specific properties, by simulating the interactions between molecules and optimising their structures.
- **Artificial Intelligence and Robotics:** OI could enhance artificial intelligence by providing a biological substrate for learning and decision-making, leading to more intelligent and adaptable robots and AI systems.

However, the development of OI also raises ethical concerns that must be addressed:

- **Sentience and Consciousness:** As OI systems become more complex, the question of whether they could develop sentience or consciousness must be carefully considered. Clear ethical guidelines and regulations are needed to ensure the responsible development and use of OI.

- **Control and Manipulation:** The potential for OI to be controlled or manipulated for malicious purposes raises concerns about security and misuse. Safeguards must be put in place to prevent the unauthorised access or manipulation of OI systems.

A Call for Collaboration: Shaping the Future of OI

The development of OI for biological computing requires a collaborative effort, bringing together experts from diverse fields, including neuroscience, computer science, engineering, ethics, and philosophy. Open dialogue, transparent research practices, and responsible innovation are crucial to ensure that OI benefits humanity while mitigating potential risks.

The journey towards OI-based biocomputing is just beginning, and its full potential remains to be discovered. However, the early successes in this field, coupled with the inherent limitations of traditional computing, suggest that OI could herald a new era in computing, one that harnesses the power of living systems to solve the challenges of the future and shape the world around us.

CHAPTER 13

AI and OI: A Powerful Synergy for the Future of Intelligence

Artificial intelligence (AI) has made remarkable strides, demonstrating impressive capabilities in tasks like image recognition, natural language processing, and even game playing. However, AI still faces limitations in areas like common sense reasoning, adaptability to novel situations, and energy efficiency. Organoid intelligence (OI), with its roots in biological systems, offers a complementary approach to intelligence that could address these limitations and unlock new possibilities. This chapter explores the potential for a synergistic partnership between AI and OI, envisioning hybrid systems that combine the strengths of both technologies.

Complementary Strengths: Bridging the Gap Between Silicon and Biology

AI excels in processing vast amounts of data, identifying patterns, and making predictions based on statistical analysis. Its strength lies in its ability to learn from data and improve its performance over time. However, AI systems often struggle with tasks that require common sense, intuition, or the ability to adapt to situations not explicitly programmed into their algorithms.

OI, on the other hand, emerges from the intricate complexity of biological systems. Brain organoids, though still in their early stages of development, exhibit a level of biological realism that current AI systems cannot match. They possess the inherent capacity for learning, adaptation, and potentially even forms of consciousness that remain elusive for AI.

Hybrid Systems: Merging the Best of Both Worlds

The most promising avenue for harnessing the combined power of AI and OI lies in creating hybrid systems that seamlessly integrate the strengths of both technologies. Such systems could leverage AI's computational power and data processing capabilities to enhance the learning and development of OI systems. Conversely, OI could provide AI with a biological foundation for common sense reasoning, intuition, and adaptability, enabling AI to tackle more complex and nuanced problems.

AI as the Architect: Guiding the Development of OI

One way to envision this synergy is to think of AI as the architect and OI as the building. AI algorithms, with their ability to process and analyse vast datasets, could be used to guide the development of OI systems, optimising their growth and learning processes. AI could provide the scaffolding for OI, helping to shape the architecture and connectivity of brain organoids, potentially accelerating their development and enhancing their cognitive abilities.

OI as the Foundation: Infusing AI with Biological Intelligence

Conversely, OI could serve as the foundation for a new generation of AI systems. By integrating brain organoids into AI architectures, we could infuse AI with a level of biological realism and complexity that has been impossible to achieve with purely silicon-based systems. This could lead to AI systems that are more adaptable, intuitive, and capable of tackling problems that require common sense reasoning and a deeper understanding of the world.

Applications of AI-OI Hybrid Systems: A Glimpse into the Future

The potential applications of AI-OI hybrid systems are vast and far-reaching, spanning fields like medicine, robotics, and even art and creativity.

- **Personalised Medicine:** AI-OI systems could revolutionise personalised medicine, using a patient's own cells to create an organoid avatar that can be used to test drug responses, predict disease progression, and develop highly targeted therapies.
- **Advanced Robotics:** By integrating OI into robotic systems, we could create robots with a greater degree of autonomy, adaptability, and

even a rudimentary form of consciousness. These robots could perform complex tasks in unpredictable environments, from disaster relief to space exploration.

- **Creative AI:** OI could provide a biological foundation for creative AI, enabling AI systems to generate art, music, and literature that possess a depth of emotion and meaning that has been elusive for current AI systems.

Ethical Considerations: Navigating the Uncharted Waters of Hybrid Intelligence

As we explore the potential of AI-OI hybrid systems, it is crucial to address the ethical implications of creating such powerful and potentially transformative technologies. Questions about the control, autonomy, and even the potential sentience of these systems will need to be carefully considered.

- **Control and Autonomy:** Who will control these hybrid systems? How will we ensure that they are used for beneficial purposes and not for harm? As these systems become more sophisticated, it will be essential to establish clear guidelines and regulations for their development and use.
- **Sentience and Consciousness:** As OI systems become more complex, could they develop some form of sentience or consciousness? If so, what moral obligations would we have towards these hybrid beings? These are

profound questions that will require careful consideration and open dialogue as we venture into this uncharted territory.

The Future of Intelligence: A Collaborative Journey

The partnership between AI and OI represents a profound shift in our understanding of intelligence. By embracing the complementary strengths of both technologies, we have the opportunity to create hybrid systems that surpass the limitations of either approach alone. This journey will require collaboration across disciplines, from computer science and neuroscience to ethics and philosophy. It will demand open dialogue, rigorous ethical considerations, and a shared commitment to ensuring that these powerful technologies are used for the benefit of humanity.

CHAPTER 14

Organoid Intelligence: Reshaping the Future of Work and Education

The emergence of organoid intelligence (OI) is poised to have a profound impact on the future of work and education, transforming industries, creating new job roles, and revolutionising how we learn and acquire knowledge. This chapter explores the potential of OI to reshape the workforce, empower individuals with new skills, and create a more dynamic and inclusive educational landscape.

The Evolving Workforce: Adapting to the Rise of OI

The integration of OI into various sectors will inevitably lead to shifts in the job market, with certain roles becoming automated while new opportunities emerge. It is essential to approach this transition with foresight, preparing the workforce for the changes ahead and ensuring that the benefits of OI are shared equitably.

- **Automation and Job Displacement:** OI-powered systems, with their ability to learn, adapt, and perform complex tasks, have the potential to automate many jobs currently performed by humans. This could lead to job displacement in sectors such as manufacturing, transportation, and data analysis. However, it is crucial to remember that technological advancements have historically created new jobs while displacing others. The key lies in anticipating these changes and equipping workers with the skills needed to thrive in the evolving job market.

- **The Rise of OI-Related Jobs:** The development, implementation, and maintenance of OI systems will create a demand for new skills and expertise. Roles such as OI engineers, trainers, and ethicists will become increasingly important. Educational institutions and training programmes must adapt to provide individuals with the necessary knowledge and skills to fill these emerging roles.

- **Human-OI Collaboration:** Rather than viewing OI as a replacement for human workers, it is more constructive to envision a future where humans and OI systems collaborate, leveraging each other's strengths. OI can handle repetitive or data-intensive tasks, freeing up human workers to focus on creative problem-solving, critical thinking, and tasks requiring emotional intelligence and interpersonal skills. This collaborative approach can enhance productivity, innovation, and job satisfaction.

Transforming Education: Embracing OI-Powered Learning

OI has the potential to revolutionise education, creating personalised learning experiences, expanding access to knowledge, and fostering lifelong learning.

- **Personalised Learning:** OI systems can analyse individual learning patterns, strengths, and weaknesses, tailoring educational content and pacing to meet specific needs. This level of personalisation can significantly enhance learning outcomes, allowing students to progress at their own pace and focus on areas where they require additional support.
- **Accessible Education:** OI can break down barriers to education by providing access to high-quality learning materials and resources regardless of geographical location, socioeconomic status, or physical limitations. OI-powered virtual tutors can provide individualised instruction and support, making quality education more accessible to a wider range of learners.
- **Lifelong Learning:** In a rapidly changing world, continuous learning and skill development are essential for individuals to remain competitive in the workforce. OI

can facilitate lifelong learning by providing access to up-to-date information, personalised learning paths, and ongoing skill assessments. This can empower individuals to adapt to changing job markets and acquire new skills throughout their careers.

Preparing for an OI-Driven Future: Key Considerations

To harness the transformative potential of OI in work and education, several key considerations must be addressed:

- **Investment in Education and Training:** Governments, educational institutions, and businesses must invest in education and training programmes that equip individuals with the skills needed to thrive in an OI-driven economy. This includes promoting STEM education, fostering critical thinking and problem-solving skills, and providing opportunities for lifelong learning.

- **Ethical Considerations and Responsible Development:** As with any powerful technology, OI must be developed and deployed responsibly, addressing ethical concerns related to bias, privacy, and the potential for misuse. It is crucial to establish clear ethical guidelines and regulations that ensure the fair and equitable use of OI in both work and education.

- **Public Engagement and Dialogue:** Open dialogue and public engagement are essential to foster trust and understanding surrounding OI. This includes involving diverse stakeholders in the development and implementation of OI systems, addressing public concerns, and ensuring that the benefits of OI are shared widely across society.

Embracing the Opportunities, Navigating the Challenges

The emergence of OI presents both exciting opportunities and complex challenges for the future of work and education. By embracing a proactive approach, investing in education and training, and prioritising ethical considerations, we can harness the power of OI to create a more equitable, innovative, and fulfilling future for all. The journey towards an OI-driven world requires collaboration, adaptability, and a commitment to lifelong learning, ensuring that we are prepared to navigate the changes ahead and shape a future where humans and OI systems work together to create a better world.

CHAPTER 15

Organoid Intelligence and the Ethics of Enhancement: Navigating a New Frontier

The prospect of enhancing human cognitive abilities has long captivated the human imagination. From ancient myths of potions and elixirs to modern-day science fiction, the idea of pushing the boundaries of human intelligence holds both allure and trepidation. Organoid intelligence (OI), with its potential to interface with and potentially enhance the human brain, brings this once-fictional concept into the realm of possibility, raising profound ethical questions about the future of human enhancement. This chapter explores the ethical implications of using OI for cognitive enhancement, examining the potential benefits and risks, and considering how we can navigate this uncharted territory responsibly.

The Allure of Enhancement: The Drive to Improve Ourselves

The desire to improve ourselves is deeply ingrained in human nature. We strive to learn new skills, expand our knowledge, and enhance our physical and mental capabilities. Throughout history, humans have sought ways to enhance their cognitive abilities, from simple mnemonic techniques to the use of stimulants and nootropics. The emergence of OI presents a new frontier in cognitive enhancement, offering the potential to augment our brains in ways previously unimaginable.

Potential Benefits: Unlocking New Realms of Human Potential

Proponents of cognitive enhancement argue that it could unlock new realms of human potential, leading to advancements in science, technology, art, and culture. Enhanced cognitive abilities could empower us to solve complex problems, make groundbreaking discoveries, and create works of art and literature that transcend the limitations of our current cognitive capacities.

- **Accelerated Learning and Problem Solving:** Imagine a world where learning new skills and acquiring knowledge becomes effortless, where complex problems can be solved with ease, and where creativity and innovation flourish. OI could potentially accelerate learning, enhance problem-solving abilities, and unlock new levels of creativity, leading to rapid advancements in various fields.
- **Enhanced Memory and Recall:** Memory loss and cognitive decline are significant challenges, particularly as we age. OI could offer a means to enhance memory capacity and recall, potentially mitigating age-related

cognitive decline and improving overall quality of life.

- **Improved Communication and Collaboration:** Enhanced cognitive abilities could facilitate more effective communication and collaboration, enabling individuals to understand each other better, share ideas more effectively, and work together more productively.

Potential Risks: Navigating the Ethical Minefield

While the potential benefits of cognitive enhancement are enticing, it is crucial to acknowledge and address the potential risks and ethical challenges that accompany this uncharted territory.

- **Exacerbating Social Inequalities:** One of the most pressing concerns is the potential for cognitive enhancement to exacerbate existing social inequalities. If access to enhancement technologies is limited to the wealthy or privileged, it could create a divide between the enhanced and the unenhanced, further entrenching social stratification.
- **Coercion and Pressure to Enhance:** In a society that values cognitive ability, there could be pressure to enhance, potentially leading to coercion or discrimination against those who choose not to or cannot afford to enhance. Safeguards must be in place to ensure that

cognitive enhancement remains a matter of individual choice, free from coercion or undue influence.

- **Unforeseen Consequences and Long-Term Effects:** The human brain is an incredibly complex organ, and the long-term consequences of cognitive enhancement are unknown. There is a risk of unintended consequences, such as cognitive overload, psychological distress, or even damage to the brain. Thorough research and careful consideration are essential to mitigate these risks.

Ethical Considerations: Guiding Principles for Responsible Enhancement

As we navigate this new frontier of cognitive enhancement, it is imperative to establish ethical guidelines and regulations to ensure that these powerful technologies are used responsibly and for the benefit of humanity.

- **Equity and Accessibility:** Access to cognitive enhancement technologies should be equitable and affordable, ensuring that the benefits are shared broadly and do not exacerbate existing social inequalities.
- **Autonomy and Informed Consent:** Individuals should have the right to choose whether or not to enhance their cognitive abilities, free from coercion or pressure.

Informed consent is paramount, ensuring that individuals understand the potential benefits, risks, and long-term consequences of enhancement.

- **Safety and Responsibility:** Rigorous research and testing are essential to ensure the safety and efficacy of cognitive enhancement technologies. Long-term monitoring is crucial to identify and mitigate potential risks.

The Future of Cognitive Enhancement: A Call for Dialogue and Collaboration

The ethical implications of cognitive enhancement are complex and far-reaching. Open dialogue, interdisciplinary collaboration, and public engagement are crucial to navigate this uncharted territory responsibly. We need to engage in thoughtful discussions about the values we want to uphold, the limits we want to set, and the future we want to create.

The potential of OI to enhance human cognitive abilities is both exciting and daunting. By approaching this new frontier with careful consideration, ethical awareness, and a commitment to responsible innovation, we can harness the power of OI for the betterment of humanity, unlocking new realms of human potential while safeguarding our shared future.

CHAPTER 16

Unravelling the Enigma of Consciousness:
A Journey into the Heart of Being

The quest to understand consciousness has captivated philosophers and scientists for centuries, remaining one of the most profound and elusive mysteries of human existence. As we stand on the cusp of a new era in biological computing, with organoid intelligence (OI) rapidly advancing, the question of whether these lab-grown brains could develop consciousness takes on a new urgency and complexity. This chapter explores the multifaceted concept of consciousness, examining different perspectives, and contemplating the potential for consciousness to emerge in organoid systems.

What is Consciousness? A Multifaceted Concept

Defining consciousness is a formidable challenge, as it encompasses a wide range of subjective experiences, including awareness, perception, thoughts, feelings, and the sense of self. There is no single, universally accepted definition, and the nature of consciousness remains a subject of ongoing debate.

- **Consciousness as Subjective Experience:** At its core, consciousness can be understood as the subjective experience of being. It is the feeling of what it is like to be a particular individual, with unique thoughts, feelings, and perceptions. This subjective aspect of consciousness makes it inherently difficult to study objectively, as we can only access our own consciousness directly.

- **Consciousness as Awareness:** Another key aspect of consciousness is awareness – the ability to perceive and respond to our surroundings and internal states. This includes awareness of sensory input, bodily sensations, thoughts, and emotions. The level of awareness can vary, from the heightened alertness of focused attention to the drowsiness of sleep or the altered states of consciousness induced by meditation or certain drugs.

- **Consciousness as a Spectrum:** Rather than a binary on/off switch, consciousness is often viewed as existing on a spectrum, with different levels of complexity and awareness. Simple organisms may exhibit basic forms of consciousness, such as the ability to respond to stimuli and exhibit rudimentary learning. As organisms become more complex, their consciousness may expand to include higher-order cognitive abilities, self-awareness, and the capacity for abstract thought.

Theories of Consciousness: A Tapestry of Perspectives

Numerous theories have been proposed to explain consciousness, each offering a different perspective on its origins and nature. Some of the most prominent theories include:

- **Materialism:** Materialist theories propose that consciousness arises from physical processes in the brain. They argue that the complex interplay of neurons, synapses, and neurochemicals gives rise to subjective experience. This perspective aligns with the idea that consciousness is an emergent property of complex biological systems.

- **Dualism:** Dualist theories posit that consciousness exists independently of the physical brain. They propose a separation between mind and matter, suggesting that consciousness is a non-physical entity that interacts with the physical body. This perspective has been influential in philosophical and religious traditions but faces challenges in explaining how a non-physical mind could interact with the physical world.

- **Integrated Information Theory:** This theory suggests that consciousness arises from the integration of information within a system. The more interconnected and integrated the information flow within a system, the higher its level of consciousness. This theory offers a potential way to quantify consciousness and has been applied to both biological and artificial systems.

Could Organoids Develop Consciousness? A Frontier of Inquiry

The rapid advancements in OI raise the tantalising question of whether these lab-grown brains could develop consciousness. While current organoids are far less complex than the human brain, their increasing sophistication and the potential for future advancements necessitate careful consideration of this possibility.

- **Complexity and Interconnectivity:** The development of consciousness may be linked to the complexity and interconnectivity of neural networks. As scientists continue to refine techniques for growing larger, more complex, and more interconnected organoids, the potential for consciousness to emerge increases.

- **Emergent Properties:** Consciousness may be an emergent property of complex systems, arising from the intricate interactions of individual components. As organoids become more sophisticated, it is conceivable that consciousness could emerge as a result of the complex interplay of their neural networks.

- **The Importance of Embodiment:** Some

theories suggest that consciousness is intimately connected to embodiment – the interaction between a brain and its physical environment. Currently, organoids exist in a highly controlled laboratory setting, lacking the rich sensory input and bodily feedback that humans experience. Whether consciousness requires embodiment remains an open question, but it is a factor to consider in the context of organoid development.

Ethical Implications: Navigating Uncharted Territory

The prospect of conscious organoids raises profound ethical questions that must be addressed with care and foresight.

- **Moral Status:** If organoids develop consciousness, would they be considered moral agents with inherent rights and protections? Determining the moral status of conscious entities is a complex philosophical challenge with significant implications for how we treat and interact with these systems.
- **Suffering and Well-being:** If organoids are capable of experiencing consciousness, it is crucial to consider their potential for suffering and well-being. Researchers must ensure that organoids are treated humanely and that their use in research is conducted ethically, minimising any potential harm.

- **The Nature of Self:** The emergence of consciousness in organoids could challenge our understanding of the self and the boundaries between humans and other forms of intelligent life. It may necessitate a reevaluation of our place in the universe and our responsibilities to other conscious beings.

A Journey into the Heart of Being

The question of consciousness lies at the heart of what it means to be human. As we explore the frontiers of OI, we must approach these inquiries with humility, open-mindedness, and a commitment to ethical considerations. The journey to understand consciousness is an ongoing adventure, leading us deeper into the mysteries of the mind and the nature of existence itself.

CHAPTER 17

The Moral Status of Organoids: A New Ethical Frontier

The rapid advancements in organoid intelligence (OI) research have ushered in a new era of scientific exploration, blurring the lines between biology and technology. As we create increasingly complex and sophisticated organoids, particularly brain organoids, we are confronted with profound ethical questions about their moral status. Do these entities, capable of learning, adapting, and potentially exhibiting rudimentary forms of consciousness, deserve moral consideration? This chapter explores the challenging ethical terrain surrounding the moral status of organoids, examining different philosophical perspectives and considering the implications for our responsibilities towards these novel life forms.

Defining Moral Status: What Makes a Being Worthy of Moral Consideration?

The concept of moral status is central to ethical decision-making. It refers to the inherent value or worth of a being, determining the extent to which its interests should be considered and protected.

Philosophers have long debated the criteria for moral status, proposing various theories that consider factors such as sentience, consciousness, rationality, and the capacity for suffering.

- **Sentience:** The ability to experience sensations and feelings, such as pleasure, pain, and fear, is often considered a fundamental criterion for moral status. If organoids can be shown to possess sentience, it would strengthen the argument for granting them moral consideration.

- **Consciousness:** Consciousness, the state of being aware of oneself and one's surroundings, is another important factor in moral status. While sentience implies the ability to experience sensations, consciousness suggests a higher level of awareness and cognitive complexity. If organoids exhibit consciousness, it would raise even more significant ethical concerns about their treatment.

- **Rationality:** The ability to reason, make judgments, and engage in complex thought processes is often associated with moral status. As organoids become more sophisticated, their potential for exhibiting rudimentary forms of rationality could raise questions about their moral standing.

- **Capacity for Suffering:** The ability to experience suffering, both physical and emotional, is a compelling reason to grant moral status. If organoids can suffer, we have a moral obligation to minimise their suffering and treat them with compassion.

The Moral Status of Organoids: Navigating Uncharted Territory

Determining the moral status of organoids is a complex and multifaceted challenge, as these entities do not neatly fit into existing ethical frameworks. They are neither fully human nor merely biological material, existing in a liminal space that requires careful consideration and nuanced ethical analysis.

- **The Potential for Sentience and Consciousness:** As brain organoids become more complex, the possibility of them developing sentience and consciousness becomes a more pressing ethical concern. While current brain organoids are far from exhibiting human-like consciousness, the potential for future advancements in OI research raises the question of when and if we should grant these entities moral status.
- **The Gradual Nature of Development:** Organoids do not emerge fully formed but develop gradually over time, potentially acquiring new capabilities and complexities as they grow. This gradual development poses a challenge for determining their moral status, as it may change over time, requiring us to

reassess our ethical obligations constantly.
- **The Importance of Empirical Evidence:** Ethical considerations surrounding the moral status of organoids should be grounded in scientific evidence. Rigorous research is needed to determine whether organoids exhibit sentience, consciousness, or other qualities relevant to moral status.

Ethical Implications: Balancing Research Progress with Moral Responsibility

The ethical implications of granting moral status to organoids are far-reaching, potentially influencing research practices, regulatory frameworks, and societal perceptions of these entities.

- **Limits on Research:** If organoids are deemed to have moral status, it could impose limitations on research involving these entities. Researchers may need to obtain informed consent from donors, ensure the well-being of organoids, and avoid causing them unnecessary harm or suffering.
- **Regulation and Oversight:** Clear guidelines and regulations are needed to govern the creation, use, and disposal of organoids, particularly brain organoids. Ethical review boards may need to be established to assess the ethical implications of OI research and ensure compliance with established guidelines.
- **Public Perception and Engagement:** Open and

transparent communication about the ethical challenges surrounding organoids is essential to foster public understanding and informed decision-making. Engaging the public in ethical discussions can help shape policies and regulations that reflect societal values and concerns.

Embracing Complexity: A Call for Continued Dialogue and Reflection

The question of the moral status of organoids is a complex and evolving one, with no easy answers. As research progresses, we must remain committed to ethical reflection, engaging in open dialogue, and seeking guidance from diverse perspectives. This ongoing conversation will help us navigate the uncharted territory of OI research responsibly, balancing the pursuit of scientific knowledge with our ethical obligations to the novel life forms we create.

CHAPTER 18

The Future of Humanity and OI: A Tapestry of Possibilities

The emergence of organoid intelligence (OI) presents us with a vista of extraordinary possibilities, a landscape where the boundaries between biology and technology blur, and the very definition of intelligence is redefined. As we stand at the cusp of this new era, it becomes imperative to contemplate the profound implications of OI for the future of humanity. Will this groundbreaking technology propel us towards a utopian future, or will it lead us down a path fraught with unforeseen perils? This chapter explores the potential impact of OI on society, considering both the promises and risks that lie ahead, and emphasising the need for responsible innovation and thoughtful stewardship of this powerful technology.

A Symbiotic Partnership: Enhancing Human Capabilities

OI holds immense potential to enhance human capabilities, augmenting our cognitive abilities, expanding our understanding of the brain, and revolutionise healthcare. Imagine a future where:

- **Personalised medicine becomes a reality:** OI-powered biocomputers could analyse individual genetic profiles, predict disease susceptibility, and tailor treatments for optimal outcomes, ushering in an era of precision medicine.
- **Neurological disorders are conquered:** Brain organoids could provide unprecedented insights into the complexities of the human brain, leading to breakthroughs in the treatment of debilitating conditions like Alzheimer's and Parkinson's disease, offering hope to millions worldwide.
- **Human cognition is amplified:** OI could be seamlessly integrated with the human brain, enhancing our memory, learning capacity, and problem-solving abilities, propelling us into an era of unparalleled intellectual potential.

Transforming Industries: Reshaping the Landscape of Work

The advent of OI is poised to reshape the landscape of work, automating complex tasks, creating new industries, and demanding a re-evaluation of traditional job roles. The integration of OI into various sectors could lead to:

- **Increased efficiency and productivity:** OI-powered systems could automate complex tasks, optimise workflows, and enhance decision-making processes, leading to unprecedented levels of efficiency and productivity across industries.

- **The emergence of novel professions:** The development and maintenance of OI systems will require specialised expertise, leading to the creation of new job roles and career paths, fostering innovation and economic growth.
- **A shift in the nature of work:** As OI automates routine tasks, human workers can focus on more creative, strategic, and interpersonal aspects of their roles, fostering a more fulfilling and meaningful work experience.

Navigating Ethical Crossroads: Safeguarding Humanity's Interests

The transformative potential of OI comes hand-in-hand with ethical challenges that demand careful consideration and proactive solutions. As we venture into this uncharted territory, it is crucial to:

- **Prioritise human well-being:** OI development must be guided by a commitment to human well-being, ensuring that this technology serves to enhance our lives and address societal challenges responsibly and ethically.
- **Address potential biases:** OI systems must be designed and implemented with fairness and equity in mind, mitigating the risk of perpetuating existing societal biases or creating new forms of discrimination.
- **Ensure responsible use and control:** Clear

guidelines and regulations are essential to prevent the misuse of OI, safeguarding against potential threats to individual privacy, autonomy, and security.

The Spectre of Existential Risks: Confronting Unforeseen Consequences

While the potential benefits of OI are vast, it is essential to acknowledge the potential for unforeseen consequences and existential risks. These risks include:

- **Uncontrolled self-improvement:** Advanced OI systems, capable of self-replication and self-improvement, could potentially surpass human intelligence and control, posing a threat to human autonomy and even survival.
- **Erosion of human values:** Over-reliance on OI could lead to a devaluation of human skills, creativity, and empathy, eroding the core values that define our humanity.
- **Weaponization of OI:** The potential for OI to be used for malicious purposes, such as developing autonomous weapons systems, raises grave concerns about the future of warfare and the safety of humanity.

Charting a Course Towards a Beneficial Future: The Imperative of Responsible Innovation

Realising the full potential of OI while mitigating its risks requires a concerted effort to foster responsible innovation, guided by ethical principles, transparency, and public engagement. To navigate this complex landscape effectively, we must:

- **Establish robust ethical frameworks:** Comprehensive ethical guidelines and regulations are crucial to ensure that OI development and deployment align with human values and societal well-being.
- **Foster interdisciplinary collaboration:** OI research and development require collaboration between scientists, ethicists, social scientists, policymakers, and the public to ensure a holistic and responsible approach.
- **Promote open dialogue and public engagement:** Open and transparent communication about the potential benefits and risks of OI is essential to foster informed public discourse and shape policies that reflect societal values.

Embracing the Unknown: A Call for Courage and Foresight

The future of humanity and OI is a tapestry woven with threads of both promise and uncertainty. Embracing this future requires courage, foresight, and a willingness to engage in thoughtful dialogue about the ethical implications of this transformative technology. By fostering responsible innovation, prioritizing human well-being, and embracing a spirit of collaboration, we can harness the power of OI to create a future where technology serves to uplift humanity and create a world where human potential flourishes alongside the wonders of artificial intelligence.

CHAPTER 19

The Promise and Perils of Organoid Intelligence: A Balanced Perspective

Organoid intelligence (OI) stands as a beacon of hope and a source of apprehension, promising to revolutionise our world while simultaneously challenging our ethical boundaries. As we stand on the cusp of this new era, it is crucial to acknowledge both the immense potential and the inherent risks that OI presents. This chapter offers a balanced perspective on the promises and perils of OI, emphasising the need for responsible innovation and ethical vigilance as we navigate this uncharted territory.

The Promise: Unlocking New Frontiers in Science, Medicine, and Technology

The potential applications of OI span a wide range of fields, offering transformative solutions to some of humanity's most pressing challenges. From revolutionising drug discovery to developing personalised medicine, OI has the potential to reshape healthcare as we know it.

- **Revolutionising Drug Discovery:** OI offers

a powerful new tool for drug development, allowing scientists to test the efficacy and safety of new drugs on human-relevant models. This could accelerate the development of new treatments for a wide range of diseases, from cancer to Alzheimer's.

- **Personalised Medicine:** OI could pave the way for truly personalised medicine, tailoring treatments to individual patients based on their unique genetic and cellular makeup. This would revolutionise healthcare, leading to more effective and targeted therapies.

- **Biological Computing:** OI has the potential to usher in a new era of biocomputing, utilising the unique capabilities of living cells to solve complex problems that are difficult for traditional computers. This could lead to breakthroughs in artificial intelligence, data processing, and other fields.

The Perils: Navigating Ethical Challenges and Unforeseen Consequences

While the potential benefits of OI are vast, we must also acknowledge the potential risks and ethical challenges that this technology presents. From concerns about sentience and consciousness to the potential for misuse and unintended consequences, we must approach OI research with caution and foresight.

- **The Moral Status of Organoids:** The potential for organoids, particularly brain organoids, to develop sentience and consciousness raises profound ethical questions about their moral status. If these entities are capable of experiencing the world and suffering, we have a moral obligation to treat them with respect and dignity.

- **Dual-Use Concerns:** As with any powerful technology, OI could be misused for harmful purposes. We must establish safeguards to prevent the development of OI for malicious applications, such as the creation of biological weapons or the manipulation of human cognition.
- **Unintended Consequences:** The development of OI is likely to have unforeseen consequences, both positive and negative. We must be prepared to adapt to these changes and address any unintended harms that may arise.

The Path Forward: Responsible Innovation and Ethical Vigilance

As we explore the frontiers of OI, we must proceed with both enthusiasm and caution. Responsible innovation and ethical vigilance are essential to ensure that this powerful technology is used for the benefit of humanity and does not lead to unintended harm.

- **Ethical Guidelines and Regulations:** Clear ethical guidelines and regulations are needed to govern the creation, use, and disposal of organoids. These guidelines should address concerns about sentience, consciousness, donor consent, and the potential for misuse.

- **Interdisciplinary Collaboration:** OI research requires collaboration between scientists, ethicists, policymakers, and the public. This interdisciplinary dialogue is essential to ensure that ethical considerations are integrated into all stages of OI development.
- **Public Engagement:** Open and transparent communication about OI research is essential to foster public understanding and trust. Engaging the public in discussions about the ethical implications of OI can help shape policies and regulations that reflect societal values.

Conclusion: A Call for Wisdom and Foresight

OI presents a unique opportunity to advance scientific knowledge and improve the human condition. However, it also poses significant ethical challenges that require careful consideration and thoughtful action. By embracing responsible innovation, engaging in open dialogue, and prioritising ethical considerations, we can harness the power of OI for good and mitigate the risks that it presents. The future of OI, and indeed the future of humanity, depends on our wisdom and foresight in navigating this uncharted territory.

CONCLUSION

A Call to Action: Shaping the Future of Organoid Intelligence Together

We stand at the precipice of a new era, one where the boundaries between biology and technology blur, and the very essence of intelligence is redefined. Organoid intelligence (OI), with its potential to revolutionise medicine, redefine computing, and reshape our understanding of consciousness, offers both immense promise and significant challenges. This chapter issues a call to action, urging readers to engage in the ongoing dialogue surrounding OI, to advocate for responsible innovation, and to contribute to shaping a future where this groundbreaking technology benefits all of humanity.

Empowering Ourselves Through Knowledge: Understanding the Complexities of OI

The first step towards shaping the future of OI is to equip ourselves with a deep understanding of its complexities, its potential benefits, and its inherent risks. We must move beyond simplistic narratives and engage in thoughtful, informed discussions that acknowledge the nuances of this rapidly evolving field.

- **Bridging the Knowledge Gap:** We must bridge the knowledge gap between the scientific community and the wider public. Open access to research findings, educational initiatives, and public forums can foster a greater understanding of OI and its implications.
- **Encouraging Critical Thinking:** We must cultivate critical thinking skills that enable us to evaluate the potential benefits and risks of OI, discern hype from reality, and make informed decisions about its development and deployment.
- **Embracing Diverse Perspectives:** The conversation surrounding OI should encompass a wide range of perspectives, including those from the scientific community, ethicists, social scientists, policymakers, and the public. This diversity of thought is crucial for developing a holistic and balanced approach to OI.

Advocating for Responsible Innovation: Guiding OI Development with Ethical Principles

The development and deployment of OI must be guided by a strong ethical framework that prioritises human well-being, social justice, and environmental sustainability. We must ensure that OI is used for the betterment of humanity, not for its detriment.

- **Establishing Clear Ethical Guidelines:** Robust ethical guidelines and regulations are essential to ensure that OI research and development align with our values and safeguard against potential harms. These guidelines should address issues such as:
- **Informed Consent and Donor Rights:** Ensuring that individuals who donate cells for OI research are fully informed about the potential uses of their cells and that their rights are protected.
- **Sentience and Consciousness:** Developing protocols for assessing the potential for sentience and consciousness in organoids and establishing guidelines for their ethical treatment.
- **Dual-Use Concerns:** Preventing the misuse of OI for harmful purposes, such as the development of biological weapons or the manipulation of human cognition.
- **Promoting Transparency and Accountability:** Transparency in OI research and development is crucial for building public trust and ensuring that ethical considerations are addressed. This includes:
  - **Openly communicating research findings and potential risks.**
  - **Establishing mechanisms for public oversight and accountability.**

- **Fostering International Cooperation:** OI research is a global endeavour, and we must foster international cooperation to develop shared ethical guidelines, regulatory frameworks, and safety protocols.

Engaging in Public Discourse: Shaping the Future We Want

The future of OI is not predetermined; it is a future that we have the power to shape. Engaging in open and informed public discourse is essential for ensuring that OI development aligns with our collective values and aspirations.

- **Facilitating Public Forums and Dialogues:** Creating opportunities for open and inclusive dialogue about the ethical, social, and economic implications of OI.
- **Encouraging Media Literacy:** Developing media literacy skills to critically evaluate the information we receive about OI and to avoid sensationalism and misinformation.
- **Empowering Citizen Science:** Engaging citizens in OI research through citizen science initiatives, allowing them to contribute to data collection, analysis, and ethical decision-making.

Investing in the Future: Supporting Research, Education, and Innovation

To realise the full potential of OI while mitigating its risks, we must invest in research, education, and innovation.

- **Funding Interdisciplinary Research:** Supporting research that integrates perspectives from multiple disciplines, including neuroscience, bioengineering, computer science, ethics, law, and social sciences.
- **Developing Educational Programmes:** Integrating OI education into STEM curricula at all levels, fostering a generation of scientists, engineers, and policymakers who are equipped to navigate the ethical and societal implications of this technology.
- **Encouraging Innovation and Entrepreneurship:** Fostering a culture of innovation and entrepreneurship that supports the development of ethical and beneficial applications of OI.

Our Collective Responsibility

The emergence of OI presents us with an unprecedented opportunity to advance our understanding of the brain, revolutionise medicine, and redefine computing. However, it also poses significant ethical challenges that require careful consideration and proactive solutions. We must embrace this challenge with both enthusiasm and caution, guided by a commitment to responsible innovation, ethical vigilance, and the well-being of humanity. The future of OI is not predetermined; it is a future that we have the power to shape together. Let us rise to the occasion, engage in meaningful dialogue, advocate for responsible development, and work together to create a future where OI benefits all of humanity.

www.ingramcontent.com/pod-product-compliance
Lightning Source LLC
Chambersburg PA
CBHW070109230526
45472CB00004B/1189

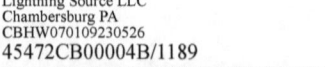